Coastal Blues

MRS. HOWARD'S GUIDE TO DECORATING
WITH THE COLORS OF THE SEA AND SKY

Phoebe Howard

ABRAMS, NEW YORK

Introduction
page 4

Sea Glass
page 8

Clear Water
page 118

Indigo Bay
page 164

Coral Reef
page 44

Deep Blue Ocean
page 82

Ocean Mist
page 196

Trade Winds
page 236

INTRODUCTION

I fell in love with blue long before I became a decorator. Growing up on the beach in Florida, I spent my days a stone's throw from the ocean, with wide-open skies above. When I was five, my mother gave in to my pleas and let me paint the walls of my room a pale aqua. I couldn't have been happier.

Decades later, as I started a design career specializing in waterfront homes, I found I wasn't alone. But my clients didn't just *like* blue, or just *love* blue. They were *obsessed* with it, especially for the interiors of their coastal properties. Very quickly, I came to understand why.

Blue connects us to nature more than any other color. But it also connects us to worlds of possibility. We gaze out at the sea, fantasizing about exotic lands, and stare up at the sky, contemplating the limitless universe. Just like the universe's unlimited potential, blue knows no bounds. Its variations and versatility are what make it so attractive to so many. Did you know that, statistically speaking, blue is the world's favorite color?

The hue can range from almost-white ice to nearly black midnight, sliding along a spectrum from grayed-out slate to supersaturated royal, turquoise to sapphire, powder to peacock. Unlike other colors, blue never runs out of ways to express itself, and in all these variations, it remains true. "Blue is the only color that maintains its own character in all its tones," the French Fauvist painter Raoul Dufy wisely noted. "It will always stay blue."

Blue's versatility equals its variety. Since different blues blend before they clash, they don't have to match to mix easily. This makes blue perfect for unifying contrasting patterns and textures. It's also forgiving: You can't make a mistake with blue. And it plays well with others. There's not a hue on the color wheel that wouldn't call blue a friend.

This flexibility extends to blue's emotional effects. Psychologists say blue calms us and puts us in an open-minded mood. There's even research suggesting it lowers blood pressure and heart rate. It turns out, blue doesn't just look good; it makes us feel good, too.

I take advantage of this constantly, often using blue through an entire waterfront house. I bring on blue, especially in lighter shades, to craft a quiet, reserved atmosphere of serenity. It makes it hard to get upset or aggressive. Stronger blues encourage reflection and stimulate clear thinking. Regardless of shade, blue feels reliable and responsible, sincere and loyal. There's a reason the expression is "true blue."

Classic and timeless, blue transcends trend, and its popularity never fades. Over the years, I've never decorated a waterfront house whose owner didn't ask for blue. I've seen how happy it makes clients in their homes, and it's been my great joy to share in that happiness.

With this book, I want to open your eyes to blue's endless decorating possibilities. I hope its pages will inspire you to dress rooms in this tried and true color in your own coastal home, experimenting with different shades and tones, playing with infinite combinations. Here, you'll discover how to swathe a space entirely in blue, how to add accents of it in small touches, and how to do something in between. You'll see rooms of all sizes, shapes, and types taking advantage of blues from across the spectrum, in myriad ways, big and small, indoors and out.

Whether decorating a beach cottage, a riverfront house, or a lakeside lodge, you'll find ways to work with coastal blues that are right for you.

Sea Glass

*Q*uite a few of my clients collect sea glass, bringing it back from the beaches by their homes to display in little bowls or jars, or to reflect its translucent blues and greens into bathroom or kitchen tiles. Often, we translate the soft hues found in a handful of sea glass into an entire interior. There's great beauty—and poetry—in reimagining something delicate that washes ashore as an interior space awash in soothing hues.

And blues and greens do truly soothe when used together. Though an old British maxim warns, "Blue and green should never be seen without a color in between," nothing could be further from the truth. The two sit right next to each other on the color wheel, so there's minimal contrast between them. It's sometimes hard to tell where blue ends and green begins, and that subtlety makes for spaces that relax and calm.

To me, and to so many homeowners, a blue-and-green palette is the most natural of choices: Every blue flower has a green leaf, after all. Sapphire waters meet verdant shores, and the sky meets the earth at the horizon. From above, our entire planet looks like an exquisitely marbleized sphere of those two hues.

PREVIOUS PAGE: *A multicolored stripe that includes a room's various hues helps unify your palette.* OPPOSITE: *Wallpaper in wide, low-contrast blue stripes softens the architecture here, while green accents ground lofty proportions.*

OPPOSITE: *The two sets of chairs flanking the sofa are of different styles, but both are covered in the same fabric. This creates a sense of implied symmetry that pleases the eye yet has more visual interest than an exact mirror image.*

13

OPPOSITE: *Warm tones of yellow-tinged greens pair especially well with cool, pale blues in this light and airy oceanfront family room. Add woven sea grass and shutter door details to enhance the beachy feel.*

14

THIS PAGE: *Why not hang inexpensive ceramic fish plates on a wall for a whimsical composition?*
OPPOSITE: *Bistro chairs with a blue-and-green diamond pattern echo the palette and lotus print of the window shades.*

Blue and green used in a subtle way—or even blended together into a single rich turquoise hue—help create a happy, cheerful space.

Who can say if the benefits of sitting outside by the sea are physical or psychological? Does it even matter?

HOW TO RELAX AND RECHARGE IN OUTDOOR SPACES

In today's fast-paced, plugged-in world, it's more important than ever to take time to relax and unwind. I can think of no better way to find a sense of inner peace and quiet than by looking out across green beach grasses to a wide-open blue sea and the distant horizon beyond. The calming effects are all but guaranteed. Here are a few easy tips for making sure your outdoor waterfront spaces are as serene as they can be—the type of place you and your family will love to come to renew, refresh, and revitalize yourselves.

BRING THE INDOOR PALETTE OUT

Make sure the colors you select for your alfresco spaces—blue and green or otherwise—play well with those in adjacent rooms. These outdoor areas will then feel more like extensions of your home and do a better job of inviting people to move outside and back in again.

STRIKE THE RIGHT NOTE WITH MEDIUM TONES

Be mindful of color outdoors. Lighter ones can get dirty quickly, and darker ones can get very hot if they are left in the sun. In-between shades are the safest bet. Sea-glass blues and greens do especially well in this medium range, and they have the benefit of reflecting the colors all around you.

REMEMBER: COMFORT IS KEY

Pick pieces that not only feel good to the touch but also make you feel comfortable. And that doesn't just mean cushions, which can be a lot of work outside. Mesh seating and Adirondack chairs are wonderful options, too—and don't forget hammocks.

GO BEYOND THE VIEW

Maximize the vistas you can see from your patio, deck, terrace, or porch, but keep in mind that at night everything changes. In the evening, you'll want seating in conversational groupings, not just facing the water.

USE A LIGHT TOUCH

You don't have to take the decoration of these spaces too seriously. Outdoor furnishings often won't last all that long, so you'll have the chance to make changes over the years, which also means you can feel free to buy less-expensive pieces. Relaxation should always be your primary focus. Let nothing impede that goal!

THIS PAGE: *Dress up an outdoor table with a beautiful tablecloth.*
OPPOSITE: *Every blue flower has a green leaf. The two hues are friends on the color wheel—and in real life.*

Dining alfresco by the water is one of life's great joys. Outdoor rooms encourage you to drink in the experience and have fun with it.

PREVIOUS PAGES: *The value of comfortable outdoor seating is undeniable, pillows and throws included.* OPPOSITE: *A corner window seat loaded with soft pillows invites you to indulge in hours of lolling about, reading, or gazing out at the sea. Blue and green work together here to become pale aqua, an appropriately watery mix.*

24

THIS PAGE: *Design a charming seaside bedroom with a shutter headboard, maritime charts, and turquoise linens.*

OPPOSITE: *What is it about a rocking motion that relaxes you on every level? Maybe it reminds us of floating in the sea.*

Rocking chairs, a porch, and a view of a blue horizon. Nothing will rest, recharge, and restore you like these simple pleasures.

OPPOSITE: *Curtains in an undulating blue-and-green print help define the perimeter of this bedroom. Other patterns and some solid fabrics pick up the palette in the rest of the space—continuing the color theme all around the room.*

28

THIS PAGE: *A burlap side chest and a rush bed provide an interesting textural touch to this bedroom, don't you think?*
OPPOSITE: *Arrange your bookcases thoughtfully, leaving space for things to breath.*

Want to add depth to bookshelves?
Paint the inside a contrasting color to the walls.
That really makes objects stand out.

OPPOSITE: *Not only do shutters look entirely appropriate in a beach house, they also accomplish the neat trick of providing plenty of privacy, while also letting in as much natural light as you'd like. They're super low maintenance, too.*

OPPOSITE: *Try contrasting textures, pairing, say, wicker chairs and woven seagrass shades with mirrored surfaces, glass, and other smooth materials.* THIS PAGE: *Periwinkle blue–and–aqua curtains in a tropical leaf–printed fabric make for a lush atmosphere in this bedroom, whose whitewashed four-poster bed is carved to resemble bamboo.*

OPPOSITE: *You can use the tiniest of touches— like the nautical artwork and blue-glass object here—to suggest a coastal atmosphere. The wallpaper, meanwhile, mimics the look of waves and becomes another reminder of nature's beauty.*

OPPOSITE: *Turquoise ceramic garden stools and palm-patterned pillows dress up this oceanfront outdoor living room. The open-weave wicker seating, meanwhile, repeats the pattern of the fretwork railings.*

Even on a chilly day, a glassed-in porch lets you enjoy the outdoors. The sun still shines through, and the right furnishings lend your space a fresh, alfresco feeling.

OPPOSITE: *Apple-green ceramic stools and all-weather wicker armchairs set with blue-and-white-striped outdoor-fabric cushions embrace a resin coffee table. These materials are especially friendly for waterfront living—essentially indestructible and easy to maintain.*

40

Sea Glass Color Palette

JET STREAM

SWISS BLUE

DOVE WING

FRASER FIR

Similarly hued blues soften bold stripes, while cream-painted trim provides crisp contrast and yellow-green a fresh complement.

BEACON GRAY

GRAND RAPIDS

SHAKER BEIGE

HORIZON

Calming and tranquil colors are ideal in a bedroom. Pairing them with ivory helps highlight the nuances of the different shades.

DISTANT GRAY   THUNDERBIRD

QUIET MOMENTS   HEALING ALOE

Misty blue and green are always appropriate at the beach, especially when combined with natural sisal, linen, and bamboo tones.

ICE MIST   ST. LUCIA SKIES

WATERCOLOR BLUE   WARREN ACRES

Muted hues tend to blend well, even in different colors, like the pale turquoises and subdued granny-smith-apple–green here.

Coral
Reef

hen casting about for a bright and bold palette to inspire your next coastal decorating project, you need look no further than the natural colors of a tropical coral reef. These vibrant underwater ecosystems teem with brilliant fish and other sea life—all in indelible, practically neon shades of pink and orange, yellow and chartreuse. Best of all, the creatures swim about against a backdrop of—you guessed it—blue. And not just any blue, mind you, but the deeply saturated sapphires and cobalts, turquoises and aquamarines of the Caribbean and the South Pacific.

This lively, high-contrast mix of hues telegraphs a feeling of excitement and electricity in any room. The warm tones radiate some sultry heat against cool blue, ensuring they look great both day and night. As a result, the palette proves itself particularly wonderful for entertaining spaces. Quite simply: It always entertains, invigorating any atmosphere. Pairing intense blues with these other hot hues stimulates the senses and makes any space feel like it's ready for a party, maybe even a bit of a boisterous one.

PAGE 45: *For a sense of youthful energy, combine complementary orange and blue.* OPPOSITE: *Outdoor fabrics and rugs in several shades of blue let this pool house work hard and play hard.*

OPPOSITE: *Make the most of a large stair landing by turning it into a casual sitting area. This one does double duty as a sleeping loft: Two guests can fit on the sectional, and the ottoman rather unexpectedly opens into a twin bed.*

49

OPPOSITE: *Periwinkle and muted orange mingle in a softer version of the coral reef scheme. Mixing different styles of seating gives your guests plenty of choices. Try a bench for overflow—it offers you more room but keeps the conversation circle open.*

50

I love using tropical flowers as a bright complement to crisp blue-and-white table settings. They enliven the atmosphere, and people find them both beautiful and intriguing.

HOW TO SET THE PERFECT WATERFRONT TABLE

I've never heard anyone complain that a table setting is too pretty. Maybe it's because I'm from the South, where we consider the craft of pairing plates with appropriate glasses, napkins with the right silver, and flowers with all sorts of accessories to be high art. But, to me, there's nothing better than a beautifully arranged table ready to welcome guests, especially on the coast. Setting the scene by the sea presents sundry opportunities—not least the chance to use blue. Read on for simple hints that make waterfront tablescaping a breeze.

TURN YOUR ATTENTION TO THE OUTDOORS

No matter how lovely your dining room or kitchen, the real entertaining action at any coastal home always happens alfresco. So put as much thought and consideration into the tables on your patio, terrace, or deck as you do those inside.

GET CREATIVE WITH CANDLES AND FLOWERS

Hurricane lanterns are always a good choice, because they protect the flame from the wind. Fill them with sand or shells to stabilize colorful candles. As for flowers, stick to local flora and then add more exotic accent blossoms, and try bowls, pitchers, and cups as vase alternatives.

CIRCLE UP AND GATHER AROUND

Smaller circular tables encourage conversation more than any other shape and limit the number of people whose backs will be to the water view. Remember: Round placemats work best on a circle, or even an oval, table.

THINK BEYOND A BLANK CANVAS

Tablecloths and napkins need not be solid. You can choose from many wonderful prints and patterns, and they take up very little space, so you can collect dozens. Since blues don't have to match to mix well together, you can feel free to try all kinds of combinations. (Avoid linen unless you love ironing!)

BRING THE SEA FLOOR TO THE TABLETOP

Salt and pepper shakers, napkin rings, vases, centerpieces, and serveware all present fantastic ways to add some under-the-sea style to your setting. Choose underwater motifs like sand dollars, starfish, and sea urchins.

THIS PAGE: *There's definitely an art to arranging an inviting bar tray. Look for colorful bottles with interesting silhouettes, and stock glasses in different shapes and sizes. Keep a shiny silver cocktail shaker on hand for a festive feel.* OPPOSITE: *When creating an alfresco table setting, take color cues from outdoor furnishings.*

OPPOSITE: *Consider concrete accents in your outdoor living area. They're durable and weatherproof, and they don't have to look industrial. The beveled corners, etched surface details, and curves in this ensemble take the edge off.*

56

OPPOSITE: *Three-dimensional art adds depth to a space. Hints of yellow in Carson Fox's floral piece mix well with a Gary Komarin painting and colorful textiles.*
THIS PAGE: *Stripes aren't just for soft goods and walls. Try them on tables and case pieces, too.*

Blue grass-cloth walls add depth and dimension to a room, creating opportunities for contrast and allowing objects to stand out.

59

OPPOSITE: *When seeking inspiration for a watery palette, you need only turn to the colors outside your seaside window. The view will provide all the hues and tones you could ever need—including the deep blues of the Teresa Bramlette Reeves artwork hanging over the sofa here.*

60

OPPOSITE: *When decorating, pick up motifs in the existing architecture. Hand-blown glass sculptures of sea life follow a circular theme established elsewhere in the room.* THIS PAGE: *A trio of round mirrors, framed in ebonized wood, echoes the rosettes on the waxed-pine antique mantel.*

PREVIOUS PAGES:
Collections needn't be
precious to be powerful.
Inexpensive beach
towels make as
dramatic a statement
as midcentury glass.
OPPOSITE: *Use strong*
color boldly but in balance.
A light-hued rug, ceiling,
and accent tables
temper saturated blues.

66

PREVIOUS PAGES:
Turquoise-colored grass cloth and framed vintage bathing suits evoke the sea.
OPPOSITE: *While not quite a color scheme you'd find on a coral reef, combining red with blue affords a similar dose of high-contrast vigor.*

There are few things as strikingly patriotic as the Stars and Stripes flying proudly in front of the sea and the sky.

OPPOSITE: *In a room with rich, saturated color, the eye needs a place to rest. White molding and wainscoting do just the trick here.* FOLLOWING PAGES: *Combine color with texture and light-catching elements on a table. Limed oak, rope, raffia, blue linen, and crackled glass form a captivating mix.*

72

THIS PAGE: *Soft fabrics and gentle curves balance hard woods and sharp edges in this sea captain's room.* OPPOSITE: *A painting of a boat's hull is a graphic alternative to more traditional nautical art.* FOLLOWING PAGES: *When weaving a color across an entire home, let some rooms use it as an accent. A drop of blue in an otherwise yellow room adds subtle charm.*

Coral Reef Color Palette

FLORAL WHITE

BEACH GLASS

MOUNT SAINT ANNE

SUCCULENT PEACH

Pair bright coral with gray blue to relax the sharp contrast between them. White walls offer a respite within the design.

SNOW WHITE

HUDSON BAY

RYAN RED

BLANCHED ALMOND

To make a red, white, and blue scheme sophisticated, use tomato instead of red and ivory instead of white. It's chic and cheerful.

PALATIAL SKIES   SAN FRANCISCO BAY

CHICAGO BLUES   WHITE DOVE

Even with white walls, a trio of strong blues gives a room a sense of depth, and makes a great backdrop for playing with bright accent colors.

RAISIN   BLUE ALLURE

COTTON BALLS   HARP STRINGS

Sunny yellow walls not only add light and happiness to a bedroom, they also provide playful contrast for splashes of bright turquoises.

Deep Blue
Ocean

*I*t may sound counterintuitive, but in waterfront spaces, I think of deep blues—from vivid royal to rich navy—as neutrals. Because black usually isn't quite right for a coastal home, these hues become the perfect choice for you to use as the darkest tones in a room. They're intense but not heavy, remaining bright and crisp, whether illuminated by daylight or by lamps and chandeliers, and they help ground a space, too.

Deep blues can create a fascinating sense of intrigue, recalling the unfathomable reaches of the ocean's depths and the mysterious pull of the wide-open sea. But they also convey affluence and strength, thanks to their affiliation with aristocracy and the monarchy. Originally derived from lapis lazuli, and first used by the Egyptians, blue has historically been the most precious and costly of pigments to produce. From ancient times up to the Industrial Age, only royalty and others with wealth and power could afford it. And that's not even how we got to royal blue specifically! It's believed *that* particular shade traces its regal provenance to Britain's turn-of-the-nineteenth-century king, George III, who asked a textile mill in Somerset to develop a hue worthy of his status. We've been benefiting from his request, and his impeccable taste, ever since.

PAGE 83: *Even in a floral print, deep blue conjures the sea.* OPPOSITE: *Though many people think the opposite is true, dark walls can cause a room to seem bigger. Corners disappear, creating a sense of expansion.*

Richly grained wood walls—like these horizontal pecky cypress boards—provide a warm and inviting atmosphere. The material perfectly balances rich blues.

OPPOSITE: *Not every room in a waterfront house has to be light and bright. Even at the beach, you'll find you occasionally want to retreat from the sun and cool off in a darker room while reading, napping, or watching movies.*

86

LEFT AND OPPOSITE:
*Art and objects should
feel personal. Collections
of shells and paintings
of whaling ships and
mermaids speak to a love
for the sea and sailing.*
FOLLOWING PAGES: *At
a beach house, a cool
blue room lets you escape
from the heat.*

Look for surprising ways to display
mementos gathered on trips to the beach.
Memories are great, but souvenirs are better.

OPPOSITE: *Lots of seating requires more room for guests to put things down. Instead of one large coffee table, why not use a pair? Doing so increases flexibility and circulation.* THIS PAGE: *Sometimes leaving windows bare is the right treatment. If you don't need privacy, it's the perfect way to soak up the view.*

OPPOSITE: *Small spaces don't necessarily require small furniture. You can deliver a sense of cozy comfort by putting an oversize sofa in a petite sitting room, just as long as you scale back the other pieces to give it a little breathing room.*

THIS PAGE: *Decorative items with clean, modern lines give traditional chinoiserie a contemporary aspect.* OPPOSITE: *Bright color can revive old favorites. Painted blue, these bamboo chairs enliven a game table, inviting guests to pull up a seat.*

Antiques needn't feel formal. Topped by simple collections, nineteenth-century chinoiserie takes on a beach-ready casual look.

OPPOSITE: *In a bright-white kitchen, scatter rich blue accents from tiles to barstools and chairs, curtains and centerpieces. These colorful moments draw attention all around the space, uniting your scheme and creating pockets of aesthetic excitement wherever you place a bit of blue.*

A backsplash is just the right spot to add a splash of blue to a seaside kitchen. Glazed ceramic or marble tiles capture the look of water and never go out of style.

HOW TO COOK UP A STORM ON THE COAST

Isn't preparing and sharing a meal with family and friends one of life's great delights? Cooking together and then feasting on the results is a wonderful way to show your affection and spend time with those you care about. A weekend or vacation house naturally lends itself to this: You and your guests have lots of downtime for browsing cookbooks, brainstorming dishes, planning menus, and prepping ingredients. And it's always more fun working as a team—especially when in a sunny, waterfront space. Here are a few ways to design a coastal kitchen that can accommodate groups big or small.

GET INTO CIRCULATION

Think about how you—and your family and guests—will move around the space. In vacation homes built for entertaining, I like the kitchen island to be a bit larger than it might be elsewhere, and I try to increase the space between countertops to provide space for many cooks in the kitchen.

DOUBLE DOWN ON APPLIANCES

Lots of cooks and lots of guests mean lots of ingredients, lots of meals, and—let's face it—lots of mess. Simplify cleanup by building in a pair of sinks, as well as two refrigerators, trash pullouts, and dishwashers.

COLOR OUTSIDE THE LINES

Kitchens offer myriad opportunities to use color well beyond backsplash tiles, wall paint, upholstery, and tabletop settings. I love blue on cabinets, whether all over or just on an island, and there are ranges and many other appliances in wonderful blue shades.

STAY HYDRATED

Refrigerated drink drawers make access to waters, juices, and sodas—not to mention beer, white wine, bubbles, and rosé—a snap. They also leave more room in the main fridge for big bowls of summer salads or marinating steaks.

BE WEAR-AND-TEAR READY

Pretty has its place in the kitchen, to be sure, but so does practicality. Avoid anything delicate or easily damaged, and use more durable materials for counters, floors, and cabinets. Making smart and appropriate decisions will put your mind at ease and let you be a better, and happier, host.

PREVIOUS PAGES: *Using similar shades of blue lets you combine several different prints and patterns.* THIS PAGE: *When it comes to selecting flowers, make hydrangeas your blue go-to.* OPPOSITE: *A blue grass cloth dining table with a teak top is equal parts pretty and practical.*

Whether you want to add contrast or a dash of color, fresh-cut flowers are always right for the dining table.

ARTFUL DECORATION INTERIORS BY FISHER WEISMAN

INSPIRED INTERIORS SUZANNE KASLER

CLASSIC *meets* CONTEMPORARY

OPPOSITE AND RIGHT:
Navy and royal both look great with tan or beige in a bedroom. Use the neutral tone for walls, curtains, and furnishings, letting the blues of patterned linens be the main event.

Pair deep blue with khaki for an ideal guestroom—nice and neutral, welcoming to both men and women, warm in winter and cool in summer.

OPPOSITE: *A slatted, distressed-oak sleigh bed resembles the hull of a ship, lending this room a nautical feeling enhanced by the convex mirror "portholes." The entire composition of light wood furnishings glows against the navy wall.*

108

OPPOSITE AND ABOVE: *Matching wallpaper and roman shades disguise the fact that the windows in this bedroom don't have ideal placement. The busy print distracts the eye.*
FOLLOWING PAGES: *Black metal and white cushions serve as a clean canvas for a simple palette of dark and light blue, reflecting the colors of the pool and the sea.*

OPPOSITE: *Sometimes natural beauty needs no enhancement. Subtle weathered wood furnishings blend with the decking here, ensuring nothing distracts from the view. Simple blue placemats, meanwhile, pick up the colors of the sea and sky.*

114

Deep Blue Ocean Color Palette

CARIBBEAN AZURE

CREAMY WHITE

VALLEY FORGE BROWN

BLUE DANUBE

Bright, almost-royal navy and natural cypress are a classically nautical combination, creating a warm, cozy, masculine look.

HASBROUCK BROWN

WINTER WHEAT

COTTON BALLS

BLUEBERRY

When using the brightest of cool blues, you can balance a room's palette by keeping the rest of your colors soft and warm.

YELLOW BRICK
ROAD

LAZY SUNDAY

CHICAGO BLUES

WINTER SNOW

*Two closely related blues get a splash
of contrast from bright yellow, while a soft
white provides a place for the eye to rest.*

WINTER WHITE

SEASIDE RESORT

PEACOCK FEATHERS

CLEAREST OCEAN
BLUE

*A mix of jewel-toned jades and sapphires
plus white adds richness and atmosphere to
this space, making it anything but ordinary.*

Clear
Water

J still remember my first trip to Hawaii, years and years ago. I was standing up to my waist in such clear water, with such pure sunlight shining overhead, I could gaze right down through the perfectly still sea to my feet. It felt like I could see every shimmering grain of cream-colored sand, every curve of each beige- and ecru-hued seashell. Glancing up, I looked back to the beach, where azure waters gently lapped against ivory shores.

My love for pairing pale blues with neutral tones—like khaki and ecru, tan and taupe—and natural materials—like raffia and wicker, grass cloth and rough-hewn wood—was born out of memories like these. The intricate textures remind me of the patterns the tide leaves on the beach and ocean floor, while the muted hues bring to mind the driftwood and shells that wash up on it. As for those light blues, they recall that ultra-clear, incredibly still water.

Juxtaposing smooth, cool blue surfaces with the relative roughness of natural materials produces intriguing contrasts. This combination of colors and textures creates a contemplative and calm atmosphere, one that's often more rustic than refined. And that makes it just perfect for a casual coastal home.

PAGE 119: *Waxed pine guarantees a rich backdrop for aqua-tinted glass objets.*
OPPOSITE: *Combine smooth-textured pale blues with tactile natural materials to suggest the appearance of the sea and sand on a calm day.*

OPPOSITE: *Arranging furniture to encourage conversation is often just as important as taking advantage of a view. Don't forget, at night, those vistas disappear.*
FOLLOWING PAGES: *Keep a room exciting by mixing pieces with interesting, mismatched wooden, wicker, and cane frames.*

122

OPPOSITE: *In a paneled room, try a light stain. You'll benefit from the warmth of wood without any of the heaviness. This is especially appropriate in a coastal home, where the pale wood looks like sand and driftwood—both of which go perfectly with many shades of blue.*

126

ABOVE: *Beach houses needn't shy away from formality.*
A grand pine doorway presents an inviting entrance to a
breakfast room. OPPOSITE: *By the sea, you'll find*
there's no flooring more apt than tiles made of coquina—
a particular type of limestone formed from crushed shells.

OPPOSITE: *When a kitchen leads right into a living space, you'll be well served to let your color palette flow seamlessly from one area to the other, so the connection between them isn't just physical but tonal, too.*

130

OPPOSITE: *A mix of formal and informal elements works well in a breakfast room, where a Chippendale cabinet and turned-leg mahogany table dress up casual sea grass and ticking stripes.*
THIS PAGE: *Antique soup tureens can serve as wonderful vases.*

Clear and blue-tinted glassware subtly suggest water and the sea, enhancing a beautifully set table.

PREVIOUS PAGE: *Art in an accent color adds a graphic pop (left), while a mix of different chairs updates the look of an antique French chestnut farm table (right).* THIS PAGE: *Vacation houses have a way of making objects gathered from all over feel right at home together.* OPPOSITE: *Light-colored open-weave rattan chairs combine with turquoise to evoke the look of driftwood washed ashore by a clear ocean.*

No shade of blue conjures the look of
a placid sea more poetically than pale turquoise—
one of the most calming of colors.

OPPOSITE: *In this casual and relaxed waterfront living room, a bit of blue goes a long way. You can use the color minimally in a mostly white space like this, and your room will still feel blue.*

138

THIS PAGE: *In a tropical climate, floor-to-ceiling French limestone keeps things cool.*
OPPOSITE: *To fit more seats around a table, choose side chairs— even oversize ones— instead of armchairs.*

Using neutrals and natural tones with blue and white softens the contrast between dark and light, creating a more soothing scheme.

OPPOSITE: *Adding midcentury pieces to your decorating mix can allow even rustic antiques to appear more modern and up-to-date. A large area rug, meanwhile, helps define an open space and adds color to stone, wood, or terracotta floors.*

142

OPPOSITE: *There's something about a turquoise room that's like a person with bright-blue eyes: Almost anything looks good on them. The energetic color goes perfectly with calm neutrals and works equally well with vivid greens, yellows, and apricots.*

145

THIS PAGE: *Even the gray hues and subtle texture of a palm's trunk can inspire a coastal decorating scheme.* OPPOSITE: *This tiny sitting room doubles as a play area for grandkids. Toys fill the wicker trunk, and the simple white sofa slipcovers can be cleaned in a snap.*

THIS PAGE: *As the modern art deco lines of these chairs prove, wicker doesn't have to look traditional.* OPPOSITE: *Let the natural surroundings inspire the design of an alfresco dining area. Here, stone, wicker, and teak recall the textures of sand, sea grasses, and the fronds and trunk of the palm tree.*

Allow oceanfront porches to pull from
the palette of the beach, capturing the colors
and textures of the sand and surf.

Diaphanous fabrics call to mind the translucence of a calm sea. Use them to fashion a canopy bed that gently envelops you and encourages restful slumber.

HOW TO SLEEP SOUNDLY BY THE SEA

Getting a good night's rest, whether at home or at a beach house, has huge health benefits. Doze with doors and windows open, the better to let in breezes and the sound of waves to lull you into blissful slumber. With fresh air, calming coastal colors, and no pressing agenda to attend to, you'll sleep better and later— and that's the best medicine you can ask for. These tips will turn your waterfront bedroom dreams into reality.

KEEP IT IN NEUTRAL

There's no more appropriate place to deploy a gentle palette of neutral hues and pale blues than a beachside bedroom. The low contrast quiets the mind and is easy on the eyes, and the light colors always stay cool, which keeps *you* cool, even in hot climates.

CONTROL THE LIGHT

Let sunshine into a room, but tame it to meet different sleep requirements. I like to install woven blinds for filtering light under curtain panels for privacy, with blackout shades underneath for complete darkness: That winning window-covering combination provides all the options you and your guests need.

DRESS BEDS IN LAYERS

I have a passion for making beautiful beds, the reward for which is restful, restorative sleep. Splurge on a feather topper and a quality mattress pad, plus decadent sheets and pillows. Layer light blankets and coverlets on top, then fold quilts and duvets at the end of the bed. An investment in these items is an investment in your well-being.

CONSIDER TEXTURE

Don't underestimate the importance of softness in a bedroom. Sisal, sea grass, and jute are beach house go-tos for rugs, and with good reason, but they may not be what you want your feet to touch at bedtime or when you wake up. Cotton, linens, and other gentle natural fibers provide a smooth and gentle feeling against your skin.

DO YOUR HOMEWORK

You spend a third of your life in bed, so you want to make the right choice. Think about options carefully: A thick mattress may be tempting but can get lumpy; organic mattresses are not treated with chemicals and do not have innersprings; and beds whose firmness and angle can be individually adjusted on each side have saved many marriages.

150

OPPOSITE: *It's no secret that light-blue bedrooms are serene, even when the color appears in multiple shades and in various patterns and textures. Experts rank the hue number one for inducing sleep.*

To make your sleeping quarters more romantic, you'll find that nothing does the trick quite like adding a canopy over the bed.

OPPOSITE: *Always think about balance: In a bedroom, seafoam walls and a pale canopy supply a soothing, feminine counterpoint to more masculine dark wood furnishings and the tactile textures of woven materials.*

154

THIS PAGE: *Consider what a mirror will reflect. Placed over an antique English pine cabinet, this seashell one aptly frames views of a beautiful beach and ocean.*
OPPOSITE: *Decorative shell accents are equally evocative whether used as a highlight (encircling a mirror or encrusting a cabinet) or as an overall theme (covering the walls of an entire powder room).*

Among nature's most beautiful wonders, seashells are all one of a kind—just like the unique homes we design for ourselves.

OPPOSITE: *Subtly patterned wallpaper can soften the edges of a room, while a fur blanket and leather-wrapped nightstands add unexpected touches of luxury.*
FOLLOWING PAGES: *With its pale aqua tones and raffia accents, this bunk room feels appropriate for both adults and kids.*

158

160

Clear Water Color Palette

WHITE DOVE

BLUE BELLE
ISLAND

WOODACRES

IVORY WHITE

*Set against the barely-there gray and
taupe hues of driftwood, a bit of bright
blue goes a long way.*

CRISP KHAKI

SEASHELL

SOFT CHAMOIS

SKYLARK SONG

*Even when relatively pale in tone, turquoise
can feel rich and full-bodied, especially when
used with ecrus and ivories.*

WHITE

PALE SMOKE

POLAR SKY

SANDY BROWN

Touches of pale, cool blues subtly accent ivory walls and the warm tones of natural materials like rope, cerused wood, and wicker.

HEALING ALOE

CHINA WHITE

MINK

GLASS SLIPPER

An unusual but restful and rejuvenating combination, grayed blue-green punctuated by ebony-brown works wonderfully in a bedroom.

Indigo
Bay

much-coveted export, indigo dye traveled on trading ships from equatorial climates for centuries, making its way to both Old World and New World fashion capitals. There, artisans used it to create beautiful textiles, and it quickly became de rigueur. Today, the color is a natural choice for a beachy look, since the tropical dye still suggests water and oceans. In fact, using it in a coastal home represents something of a homecoming.

Indigo's broad range of hues—between pure blue and pure violet on the color spectrum—are wonderfully suggestive of the sea. The variegated feel, finish, and often faded look of indigo-dyed fabrics recall waves and whitecaps, as well as the variety of blue shades you see when you look across the ocean or gaze into the water.

Indigo has true international appeal, too, equally associated with the batiks and tie-dyes of Indonesia, the paisleys and woodblocks of India, and—let's not forget—those all-American blue jeans. When you decorate with indigo, you can just as easily allude to the casual, hardworking aesthetic of domestic dungarees, the artistry and craft of Asia, and the romance and mystery of the sea.

PREVIOUS PAGE: *Design a dramatic vignette using oversize pieces.* OPPOSITE: *Antiques, like this Biedermeier secretary and English mantel, imbue a room with historic patina, while indigo accents signal a sense of tall ships and sea trade.*

Indigo-dyed textiles, especially block prints and batiks, can lend a room an international flavor, one that hints at intrepid explorations of remote destinations.

OPPOSITE: *A global mix of treasures helps a space tell stories that span generations and time zones, while vibrant blue-and-white accents refresh antiques and souvenirs alike.* FOLLOWING PAGES: *Using the same print on several items in a room keeps a decorating scheme from becoming too busy.*

OPPOSITE: *Antique
wicker and a vintage-
inspired slipper chair get
a contemporary update
thanks to brightly hued
indigo fabrics. A mix
of nautical paintings and
dioramas displayed in
a grid with plenty of
white space completes
the old-meets-new look.*

172

THIS PAGE: *Keep custom decorating details personal. This sailor's valentine was made on the island of Bequia by artists Sam and Donna McDowell. The scrimshaw in the middle is a replica of the homeowners' sailboat, the* Seahawk. OPPOSITE: *The ship's wheel motif of the Windsor chair picks up the maritime theme of the artwork.*

In the living or family room of a casual beach house, you always want to make it easy to relax and get comfortable.

HOW TO GATHER WITH COMFORT AND EASE

As much time as you, your family, and friends spend *outside* at a coastal home, there are plenty of reasons to come *indoors*, too. So it's vital to have a cozy, welcoming space for playing games, watching movies, cheering for your favorite team, and enjoying cocktails and conversation when it's wet or cold out. Here are some helpful hints for making group hangout spots as convivial as possible.

GET IN THE MIDDLE OF THINGS

You want your main gathering space to be in, or at least near, the center of a home, so all activity can flow from it. Let your color palette do the same, making its way out from this hub. If you're weaving indigo throughout your house, let it be at its strongest here.

DO THE MATH

Have enough seating to accommodate a full house: If your home can sleep twelve people, you should have perches for at least that many. This rule extends to ottomans and tables, too. You want the space to feel generous, so that everyone has a spot to put their feet up or glasses down.

MAXIMIZE FLEXIBILITY AND FLOW

Beach houses accommodate gatherings great and small, and rooms are often used in myriad ways—living room one minute; sleeping porch the next. Swivel chairs and lightweight rockers let you reconfigure things with ease, as do portable and folding chairs for when there's a crowd. A large sofa or sectional may seat more people, but it can make it hard for guests to circulate. Consider smaller furnishings in several groupings.

DON'T UNDERRATE DURABILITY

Gathering spaces should be all but indestructible. Outdoor fabrics now mimic indoor materials—cottons, linens, velvets—and there are beautiful water-resistant leathers, too. Distressed wood, shagreen, and painted surfaces can all withstand a lot of wear and tear, and I love using ceramic garden stools as waterproof drinks tables.

HIDE THAT TV

A television doesn't have to be the focal point. You can conceal flat screens behind artwork, mirrors, or cabinet doors. At the touch of a button, a TV can rise from a trunk, credenza, or cabinet. A framed recessed niche also goes a long way toward giving a wall-mounted television a finished look.

OPPOSITE: *Inherited from the home's previous owners, this beautiful antique pine paneling was imported from Europe and fitted to this space. Talk about a bonus room!*
FOLLOWING PAGES: *Indigo hues can unify an oddly shaped room's quirky angles and dimensions.*

178

OPPOSITE: *Vivid hues of blue are balanced by the warmth of rope, driftwood, sea grass, and wicker. And who doesn't love a banquette? It's a great way to add comfort to your dining experience.*

182

OPPOSITE: *Think beyond wallpaper: A decorative painter created this small print by hand, directly onto the wall.* THIS PAGE: *Layer windows with curtains and blinds in various materials. These options can let in more or less light, and offer two different looks.*

OPPOSITE: *Faux bois wallpaper lends coziness to this TV room, warmth that's balanced by cool indigo touches.*
FOLLOWING PAGES: *Striped wallpaper on the ceiling, with a coordinating color on the walls, expands the sense of space in a low room (left). The convex mirror (right) has a similarly space-enlarging effect.*

THIS PAGE: *A chaise longue is all the invitation you need to linger poolside.*
OPPOSITE: *Wicker baskets keep open shelves tidy in a mudroom.*
FOLLOWING PAGES: *Classic indigo stripes and block prints can read as nautical or modern, and are always classic.*

A pool surrounded by natural bluestone
gives you and your home a connection to the
water, whether you're on the coast or not.

Indigo Bay Color Palette

PEBBLE BEACH

MIDDLEBURY BROWN

PHILIPSBURG BLUE

WHITE DOVE

In this kitchen, indigo cabinets and light-blue walls cause your eyes to focus on the unexpected colors instead of the odd angles.

BRIDGEWATER TAN

OLD BLUE JEANS

SEA VIEW

DECORATOR WHITE

Different shades of indigo-dyed denim always go well together, and they look great with a variety of other blues and neutrals, too.

194

ALASKAN HUSKY   HORIZON

CHINA WHITE   BLUE HEATHER

Dark hues on the floor and furniture and pale hues on the walls and ceilings help a low space seem loftier than it is.

GLASS SLIPPER   NEW PROVIDENCE NAVY

WHITE   SEASHELL

Create a sense of expansion in a compact space by bookending pale blue with darker floors below and white ceilings above.

195

Ocean
Mist

I have yet to meet a person who doesn't love looking out at the horizon. Contemplating the place where the sea meets the sky at its palest point becomes an almost meditative experience, freeing and opening your mind to ruminate and reflect. You can easily achieve the same sort of creative and enlightened feeling in your own home, simply by decorating with the lightest of misty blue hues.

Promoting feelings of peace and tranquility, calm and serenity, this palest of pale tones suggests a heavenly or spiritual atmosphere, and it has wonderfully celestial connotations. Just think of its traditional use on porch ceilings, where it recalls the sky. The oh-so-soft color also represents health and healing. For all these reasons, it's fantastic in a bedroom, where it soothes and quiets your mind at bedtime and when you first wake up. As appealing to men as to women, it works equally well in busy, high-traffic areas, where it can mitigate our contemporary, always-on-the-go lives. So, next time you're considering pure white for a wall, add a hint of blue into that can of paint and, with it, a sense of bliss.

PREVIOUS PAGE: *Touches of misty blue on fabrics and in bedding lend even the most formal furnishings a casually elegant air.* OPPOSITE: *Soft shades of blue and ivory make a dressy room tranquil.*

OPPOSITE: *Not just color but also texture can contribute to a seaside feeling. The bleached ivory–hued seagrass rug, stone coffee table, painted side tables, and, perhaps most of all, the strié wallpaper work together to evoke coastal mists and clouds.*

200

OPPOSITE: *In a home designed for both owners and seasonal renters, textiles, rugs, and furnishings had to be sturdy enough to withstand wear and tear. That meant outdoor fabrics in forgiving beige and gray stripes, instead of white and ivory or solid colors.*

OPPOSITE: *Even when you base a color scheme on pale blue, you can find a place for brighter hues. Here, a graphic rug adds bold dimension, acting as a work of art amid the more neutral tones.*

205

OPPOSITE: *Only the very palest of pale blues were used here, with white and a variety of textures. The palette is intended to frame—and not detract from—the intense colors of the beach views just beyond the windows.*

206

Stair risers present a prime opportunity to make a statement: Try using paint, tiles, or wallpaper—no runner required.

OPPOSITE: *Lovely to look at and equally great to actually use without fear of damage, all the fabrics in this sky-blue family room—including the delicate-seeming sheer window treatments—are made of stain-resistant indoor-outdoor materials.*

210

OPPOSITE: *A four-poster bed and tall, white-painted wainscoting—which provide contrast to the light-blue walls—keep this large, high-ceilinged bedroom feeling warm, cozy, and intimate.*

OPPOSITE: *The juxtaposition of deeply colored woods with light blue keeps this living room grounded and crisp. As long as you select and place them strategically, you can add darker elements into a pale room and still produce a soft, calm space.*

214

Light blue soothes the soul and relaxes the mind, encouraging daydreaming and contemplation. Playing cards or a low-stakes board game has a similar effect.

HOW TO PLAY NICELY NEAR THE SHORE

In our ever-more on-call lives, it has gotten harder and harder to turn away from our smartphones, tablets, and computers. As a result, we're missing opportunities to engage in the real-life interactions with family and friends that most enrich us. But there is hope! Game tables in homes are popular once more, helping us unplug from technology and reconnect with one another. Here are my top tips for creating a good old-fashioned game area in your home.

FIND YOUR PLACE

Game tables aren't just for dens or family and living rooms. In a spare bedroom or home office, they do double duty as desks, and in a kitchen or dining area, they're handy for additional table space, should extra guests show up.

TURN THE TABLES

I prefer square game tables to round ones, because I like to place them in corners, at a 45-degree angle to the walls. This creates space all around for chairs and players, and it adds a bit of a surprise to a floor plan. (Square tables can prevent your friends from peeking at your cards, too.) In terms of size, thirty-six inches works well for most

activities, though you may want something more like forty-eight for puzzles.

TAKE A SEAT

Chairs matter always, but especially at a game table, where you may be sitting and leaning in for hours. The pieces you pick should have arms, and those arms should fit under the table. You'll want comfortably upholstered seats and backs, rather than wood or another hard surface.

DRINK IN THE FUN

Games are somehow always more enjoyable with a beverage—whether a soft drink, cocktail, or glass of wine. I like to place a drinks cart near the area where we'll be playing, stocking it with a variety of things to sip and snack on. Certain game tables have built-in, pullout drinks holders—a particularly genius detail.

LIGHT UP THE NIGHT

You've got to have good lighting. This doesn't have to mean placing a pendant directly overhead. I've often tucked a floor lamp into the space next to a game table, which more than adequately illuminates things. Adjustable swing-arm styles work especially well.

216

OPPOSITE: *Gauzy fabrics require more volume to look full. When using translucent textiles for curtains, have each panel be at least three times the window's width. Sheers don't offer much light control, so consider adding blinds or shades behind.*

THIS PAGE: *A lovely oval window presented a great opportunity to echo its curves throughout this room, in the headboard, for example, and bedside lamps, too.*
OPPOSITE: *The smallest of details adds character. Delicate hand embroidery along the borders and across the hems of these curtain panels enhances the entire space.*

OPPOSITE: *Use geometric tilework to revive a tired wall.*
THIS PAGE: *A green glass chandelier over a bleached-wood table recalls the bottles on display nearby.*

Pale blue pairs beautifully with light wicker and bleached wood, creating a tranquil, airy atmosphere.

223

OPPOSITE AND ABOVE: *Let architecture guide you. A bed whose posts align perfectly with windows looks custom made for this room.* FOLLOWING PAGES: *To create flow, you sometimes need only weave a thread of a color from room to room.*

OPPOSITE: *The repeating curves of the headboard, bedside lamps, and curtain valance create a sense of rhythm.*
THIS PAGE: *A mirror on the wall opposite a bed lets you see what hangs above the headboard, even when you're leaning against it.*

Let beauty take the lead, especially in a bedroom. The loveliest and most restful sleeping spaces have pale and peaceful palettes.

OPPOSITE: *No matter how stunning the view, you likely still want window treatments, especially in a bedroom. Here, pleated sheer roman shades filter light and provide privacy when necessary.*

231

LEFT AND OPPOSITE: *Try adding oversize drawer pulls and cabinet handles to bathroom vanities. They're a great way to keep your space feeling current and interesting.*

Whether you use it on walls or on cabinets, pale blue sets a clean, refreshing tone that's exactly right for your bathroom.

Ocean Mist Color Palette

CHANTILLY LACE

PEARL GRAY

SLEIGH BELLS

FRENCH CANVAS

Delicate, almost-white shades that are mere whispers of color mix nicely, especially in a space designed to be soothing.

HINT OF MINT

HAWAIIAN BREEZE

GLACIER WHITE

EMERALD VAPOR

The palest of pale blues and greens are particularly easy on the eyes, and a dream to blend in various different combinations.

234

BREATH OF FRESH AIR

EDGECOMB GRAY

REVERE PEWTER

FANFARE

Even in a very subtle palette, try adding one brighter color. Doing so throws dark and light into wonderful relief.

WHITE DOVE

GLASS SLIPPER

QUIET MOMENTS

MIDDLEBURY BROWN

The contrast provided by a single darker, deeply colored neutral helps paler hues show themselves off in the best light.

235

Trade Winds

lue and white is the only color combination I come back to time and again. Not blue with something else, not white with another hue—not even black. If you're like me, you just can't get enough blue and white, and you can't be swayed otherwise. What is it about this palette that gives it such widespread appeal and inspires such devotion?

To start, there's the fact that blue is the world's favorite color. Found all around us in nature, it knows no limits when it comes to a particular fashion or style, time period or geography. As for white, it shows blue off in its truest form, without distraction or competition. And though it delivers plenty of contrast, the combination is less stark than black and white. It's easy on the eyes. White sets blue up for success, which sets you and your decorating scheme up for success, too.

This high-contrast, timeless combination always looks fresh, even though it's rooted in history: The Western world has been obsessed with this crisp mix at least since the fourteenth century, when Chinese porcelain arrived in Europe. Used in trading ships as ballast, the ceramics spread to the colonies, becoming all the rage. Centuries later, blue and white feel as of the moment as ever.

PREVIOUS PAGE: *To really make them pop, place pieces of Chinese export porcelain within an otherwise black-and-white palette.* OPPOSITE: *When decorating a room in similar blues, play with the proportion and scale of different prints.*

OPPOSITE: *Blue can have a big impact even when used in relatively small ways. In this predominantly white family room, an azure-striped rug and pillows embellished with sapphire patterns invite the colors of the pool terrace indoors.*

240

Your room can
easily become a
beautiful melting
pot of blue. Various
shades and tones,
solids and patterns,
all blend seamlessly.

OPPOSITE: *In an architecturally ordinary
space, create intrigue with a sea of global
blue-and-white prints.* FOLLOWING
PAGES: *Ikats and chinoiserie screens pick
up the blues of export porcelain, ensuring
that everything harmonizes nicely.*

242

LEFT AND OPPOSITE: *When arranging shelves, start with ceramics, creating symmetry and rhythm, then fill the empty spaces with books and other objects.*

Authentic or reproduction, blue-and-white ceramics always have appeal. You don't need to be a connoisseur to get the look.

Classic Chinese blue-and-white
porcelain can be used as a decorative
accent, a tabletop setting, or the
pattern that wraps an entire room.

OPPOSITE: *The combination of robin's-egg strié panels with custom wall
murals—commissioned from Savannah, Georgia–based artist Bob Christian—
creates a magical atmosphere in this dining room.* FOLLOWING PAGES: *These
murals resemble glazed blue-and-white porcelain and echo favorite
ports of call, including Florida and South Carolina.*

THIS PAGE: *An
Anglo-Indian cabinet
handsomely hides a TV.*
OPPOSITE: *For a
mealtime setting as
cohesive as it is dynamic,
collect different bold
patterns of similarly
colored tabletop pieces.*

Celebrate wanderlust by combining elements
from different cultures, places, and periods.
Armchair travel never looked so good!

PREVIOUS PAGES: *Let the colors of a dining room's decoration and artwork be your muse when you set the table.* THIS PAGE: *A banquette, chairs, and garden stools create an inviting space for pre-dinner drinks in a dining room.* OPPOSITE: *On the table, think in layers—placemats, chargers, plates, and bowls all add dimension, color, and pattern.*

256

> When you love grand views of ocean and clouds, blue and white becomes a combination you'll always crave, especially in a dining room. It's just so delicious.

HOW TO DINE CASUALLY ON THE COAST

At a waterfront vacation house, savoring a long, lovely lunch or dinner is often one of your day's primary goals. The pace of life seems to slow down, and it feels like you're never short on time when you're sitting around a table with family and friends, enjoying good food and spirited conversation—ideally sans cell phones. These moments surely enhance and even extend our lives. To help you have more of them, here are a few tips for planning a casual coastal dining area you'll want to linger in.

EXPAND THE POSSIBILITIES

Round tables can be wonderful, but for a circle to fit a lot of people, it often must be so big that your guests may have difficulty talking across it. If you'll be hosting larger groups, consider a rectangle, or a circle whose leaves turn it into a long oval. (As for the seats, I prefer chairs with arms. They increase everyone's comfort.)

GO TO PRINT

Placing a pattern on chairs makes a bigger impact than using it elsewhere in a room—on curtains, say, where the print might be hard to see. A pattern has the added benefit of hiding stains and handling wear and tear well, even more so if you have it printed on an outdoor fabric, as I often do.

SKIP THE RUG

I love beautiful carpets and appreciate how they can ground and add color and life to a room. In a casual coastal home, however, I like to leave the floor bare in the dining area. Not only does this save you time and hassle when it comes to cleanup, it keeps things cool underfoot, even in hot climates.

SOFTEN THE SOUND

Since you'll be skipping the rug, it's important to layer in other textiles to dampen voices and echoes so your guests can hear each other talk. In addition to upholstered or slipcovered armchairs in a dining room, curtains also help control the volume.

FIND YOUR LIGHT

For a dining area, I always prefer a chandelier or a pendant over recessed lighting. The piece's width should be less than seventy-five percent of your table, and it should hang thirty-six to forty inches above the tabletop. Put it on a dimmer to create the most flattering glow.

PREVIOUS PAGES: *In a kitchen, glass tiles in a Moroccan shape lend a handcrafted quality.* LEFT AND OPPOSITE: *Bright yellow captivatingly complements blue and white, bringing a warm, sunny presence.*

A poolside breakfast always sets the stage for a day of fun in the sun, encouraging guests to linger and lounge at their leisure.

ABOVE AND OPPOSITE: *Comfortable furniture invites you to really use your alfresco space. Several manufacturers now sell upholstered and slipcovered items designed to withstand the elements.* FOLLOWING PAGES: *Larger blue-and-white ceramics serve as ideal outdoor tables.*

Trade Winds Color Palette

CALM

STRATFORD BLUE

ADMIRAL BLUE

VANBUREN BROWN

*Blue and white never look better
than when displayed without distraction
or competition on a dark surface.*

MYSTICAL BLUE

CHINA WHITE

OAKWOOD MANOR

BAYBERRY BLUE

*Stretching blue along the tonal spectrum
from pale to bright is a wonderful way to
develop a palette for a room.*

268

HEAVEN ON EARTH   ACADIA WHITE

POOLSIDE   ICE CAP

A mix of robin's egg, cobalt, sapphire, and light blues shows how well various shades of the color can all work together.

DALILA   LAKE TAHOE

PARTY PEACH   KIWI

A Chinese ceramic palette needn't end with blue and white. The combination makes a great foil for other bright colors found in nature.

269

ACKNOWLEDGMENTS

While working on each of my books—this is my third—I have grown and learned in different ways, as a new set of challenges and opportunities presents itself. One thing remains the same every time, however: It takes a lot of people to create a decorating book. I couldn't have managed this project without a very talented team, and I'd like to extend my heartfelt thanks to everyone who helped me with it.

My publisher, Abrams, and especially Shawna Mullen, my insightful and supportive editor there, believed in me and gave me another opportunity to record my work and express myself. For that, I am extremely appreciative. Thanks also to the whole Abrams team: managing editor Mary O'Mara, design manager Danny Maloney, and assistant editor Emma Jacobs. Visionary book designer Doug Turshen and his right-hand man, Steve Turner, made the process incredibly easy. I especially love their candor and honesty when they tell me something just isn't good enough to include! I feel lucky to have found the talented writer Andrew Sessa to help me with the text for this book. Smart and easy to work with, he amazed me with his brilliant grasp of language. He has a beautifully poetic way with words.

In a book like this, the photography is just as important as those words, maybe even more so. The images convey the story I want to tell, inviting readers in and allowing them to dream and be inspired. I've enjoyed working with all the talented photographers I've collaborated with, many of whose pictures are included here. But Josh Gibson, who I have known for years and who I am now happy to call my good friend, deserves special notice.

My husband and partner, Jim Howard, and I have been married for thirty years and in business together for twenty. The body of work Jim and I have created is something special—and so is our bond. I couldn't have chosen a better man to spend my life with.

I am in the very fortunate position of having our daughter Nellie Jane join our design and retail business. To watch her grow and to see her talent developing is a special gift, as was the assistance and the insight she offered me on many of the projects featured in this book. A design force in his own right—whose interiors have appeared on many magazine covers—our son Andrew has long been Mr. Blue. From him I've learned invaluable lessons about using the color in creative and interesting ways. A final family thank-you goes to my mother, Madeline McGinty, who has always been there to motivate and encourage me; she is one of a kind.

I owe my wonderful and trusting clients a huge debt of gratitude for inviting me into their worlds and allowing me to be such a large part of their lives. It is a special privilege for me to get to work with all of them, sometimes on several of their houses. Two clients deserve a particularly special thank-you: Without Tricia and Ben Carter, I would never have written a book about blue. They introduced me to the absolute wonders of the color, helping me see the various ways it can so beautifully reflect the sea and sky. I feel very fortunate to have had the opportunity to decorate many different houses for these true blue experts.

Last but certainly not least, I must also thank my loyal and fabulous employees, who make all of these projects happen. Without them, I would be nothing! They continue to inspire me and make me laugh every day, and for that I am eternally grateful.

All photographs credited © Josh Gibson except where noted below:

©Danny Barley (p. 8, 44, 82, 118, 164, 196, 236); ©Roger Davies (p. 239); ©Spencer J. Fisher (p. 108-109, 212-213); ©Tria Giovan (p. 17, 27, 45, 112-113, 132, 136, 157 [bottom left], 180-181, 190-191, 208); ©Laurey W. Glenn (p. 50-51, 224-225); ©Robbie Hickman (p. 24-26); ©James Lockheart (p. 76, 167-169); ©Laura Moss (p. 5, 64-65, 188); ©Jessie Preza (p. 133); ©Frances Ann Spurling (p. 140, 189)

Benjamin Moore®

Paint colors in the Color Palette sections used with permission from Benjamin Moore®.

SEA GLASS COLOR PALETTE (p. 42) Jet Stream 814, Swiss Blue 815, Dove Wing 960, Fraser Fir 503, Beacon Gray 2128-60, Grand Rapids 835, Shaker Beige HC-45, Horizon 1478, (p. 43): Distant Gray 2124-70, Thunderbird 675, Quiet Moments 1563, Healing Aloe 1562, Ice Mist 2123-70, St. Lucia Skies 781, Watercolor Blue 793, Warren Acres 527

CORAL REEF COLOR PALETTE (p. 80) Floral White OC-29, Beach Glass 1564, Mount Saint Anne 1565, Succulent Peach 068, Snow White OC-66, Hudson Bay 1680, Ryan Red 1314, Blanched Almond 1060, (p. 81): Palatial Skies 800, San Francisco Bay 802, Chicago Blues 804, White Dove OC-17, Raisin 1237, Blue Allure 771, Cotton Balls OC-122, Harp Strings 213

DEEP BLUE OCEAN COLOR PALETTE (p. 116) Caribbean Azure 2059-20, Creamy White OC-7, Valley Forge Brown HC-74, Blue Danube 2062-30, Hasbrouck Brown HC-71, Winter Wheat 232, Cotton Balls OC-122, Blueberry 2065-30, (p. 117): Yellow Brick Road 349, Lazy Sunday 803, Chicago Blues 804, Winter Snow OC-63, Winter White 2140-70, Seaside Resort 725, Peacock Feathers 724, Clearest Ocean Blue 2064-40

CLEAR WATER COLOR PALETTE (p. 162) White Dove OC-17, Blue Belle Island 782, Woodacres 1020, Ivory White 925, Crisp Khaki 234, Seashell 926, Soft Chamois OC-13, Skylark Song 778, (p. 163): White OC-151, Pale Smoke 1584, Polar Sky 1674, Sandy Brown 1046, Healing Aloe 1562, China White OC-141, Mink 2112-10, Glass Slipper 1632

INDIGO BAY COLOR PALETTE (p. 194) Pebble Beach 1597, Middlebury Brown HC-68, Philipsburg Blue HC-159, White Dove OC-17, Bridgewater Tan 1096, Old Blue Jeans 839, Sea View 836, Decorator White OC-149, (p. 195): Alaskan Husky 1479, Horizon 1478, China White OC-141, Blue Heather 1620, Glass Slipper 1632, New Providence Navy 1651, White OC-151, Seashell 926

OCEAN MIST COLOR PALETTE (p. 234) Chantilly Lace OC-65, Pearl Gray 863, Sleigh Bells 1480, French Canvas OC-41, Hint of Mint 505, Hawaiian Breeze 772, Glacier White OC-37, Emerald Vapor 845, (p. 235): Breath of Fresh Air 806, Edgecomb Gray HC-173, Revere Pewter HC-172, Fanfare 874, White Dove OC-17, Glass Slipper 1632, Quiet Moments 1563, Middlebury Brown HC-68

TRADE WINDS COLOR PALETTE (p. 268) Calm OC-22, Stratford Blue 831, Admiral Blue 2065-10, Vanburen Brown HC-70, Mystical Blue 792, China White OC-141, Oakwood Manor 1095, Bayberry Blue 790, (p. 269): Heaven on Earth 1661, Acadia White OC-38, Poolside 775, Ice Cap 1576, Dalila 319, Lake Tahoe 783, Party Peach 139, Kiwi 544

The publisher has made best efforts to faithfully reproduce approved Benjamin Moore paint swatches. However, due to the natural color variations that occur when using CMYK printing to reproduce the paint swatches, the paint samples in this book should not be viewed as substitutes for the Benjamin Moore swatches. For authentic Benjamin Moore colors and paint swatches, please visit your nearest Benjamin Moore retailer.

Editor: Shawna Mullen
Designer: Doug Turshen with Steve Turner
Production Manager: Denise LaCongo

Library of Congress Control Number: 2016941893

ISBN: 978-1-4197-2480-0
eISBN: 978-1-68335-227-3

Text copyright © 2018 Phoebe Howard

Printed and bound in China

12

Abrams books are available at special discounts when purchased in quantity for premiums and promotions as well as fundraising or educational use. Special editions can also be created to specification. For details, contact specialsales@abramsbooks.com or the address below.

ABRAMS The Art of Books
195 Broadway, New York, NY 10007
abramsbooks.com

boca grande 26°44'n 82°15'w